M000200033

Published in the United States by Bits of Steak Press, Alameda, California

Paperback ISBN 978-1-7351080-4-9
Hardcover ISBN 978-1-7351080-6-3
eBook ISBN 978-1-7351080-5-6

Cover design by Graye Smith
Edited by Jessica Berbey
Typesetting by Vanessa Mendozzi

Publisher's Cataloging-In-Publication Data
(Prepared by The Donohue Group, Inc.)

Names: McNair, Randall, author.
Title: Make it a double : more poems from my 10-year bender inside heaven's
    dive bar / Randall McNair.
Description: Alameda, CA : Bits of Steak Press, [2021] | Series: [Bar poems] ; [2]
Identifiers: ISBN 9781735108049 (paperback) | ISBN 9781735108063
    (hardcover) | ISBN 9781735108056 (ebook)
Subjects: LCSH: Alcohol--Poetry. | Life--Poetry. | Death--Poetry. | American
    poetry. | LCGFT: Humorous poetry. | Poetry.
Classification: LCC PS3613.C58574 M35 2021 (print) | LCC PS3613.
    C58574 (ebook) | DDC 811/.6--dc23

MAKE IT
A
DOUBLE

**More poems from my 10-year
bender inside heaven's dive bar**

RANDALL MCNAIR

Bar Poems – Book 2

Alameda, CA

ACKNOWLEDGMENTS

For my brother, Scott, whose witty, wisecracking, whiskey-loving ways taught me so much about living and writing that I would be a lifeless mute without him. So yeah, you have him to blame for this.

And, as in *Dispatches*, I must acknowledge the master himself—here's a tilt of the mug to Charles Bukowski, whose countless books of poetry kept me company on many a barstool during my decade-long bender at the Swinging Door Saloon.

Cheers, Scotty! Prost, Buk!

Finally, grateful acknowledgment is made to the editors at Blood & Bourbon, who first published "Whiskey Dick" in their Issue #7.

DISCLAIMER

This is not
your mother's poetry—
erudite and finished.

No, this is swinging-dick poetry,
big-hanging-balls poetry,
written by a man for men.

Did your mother ever
tell you
to watch your mouth?

Well, don't you worry about that here, Stranger.
Profanity proliferates on the pages
of my poetry.

This is broken-tooth,
busted-ribs, knife-to-the-gut,
HOLY-SHIT, oh-no-he-DIDN'T poetry.

This is whiskey-dripping-from-your-beard
poetry, the-smell-of-pussy-stuck-to-your-mustache
poetry.

And, while I'm sure your mother
wrote some amazing shit, I'll bet
she never wrote a poem entitled *Whiskey Dick*.

And, as for my indelicate use of words
like "pussy" and "dick," go suck one.
Because I am a man, and this is *my* shit.

MAKE IT A
DOUBLE

Contents

The Status Quo

Make it a Double	3
Another Goddamn Sales Meeting	5
Whiling Away the Day	6
Channeling Bukowski	7
I Write Love Poems	8
Herpes—a Love Story	11
An Ode to Tits	12
Like a Cloud in August at Noon	13
Scratching an Itch	14
Drunk Genius	15
Iron Man	16
These are my Books	18
Run with the hunted	20
Disappointment	22
Clone	23
The Annoying Guy	24
Inventory Shrinkage	25
Never Trust your Drinking Tutelary inMatters of Life and Death	26
These Goddamn Hoopties	28
Her Eyelashes	30
Beer Battered and Twice Cooked	31
This Whole Filthy World	33
A Simple "Thank you" Would Have Sufficed	35
Conversation with a friend	36
Eighty Dollars Ago	37
Aging	38

THE DESCENT

Whiskey I	41
Consumption	42
Losers like Us	43
I Cried Today	45
Here's What You Should Do	47
A Lonely Drunk	49
Negative Self-Talk #1	50
Negative Self-Talk #2	51
Trouble is Brewing	53
Our Heads into the Mouth of the Beast	54
The Dirty Rag of Living	56
The Biggest Drunk I Ever Met	57
48 Hours in the Tank	59
My Wife	60
She is the Dawn	61
Drinking the Purpose Away (Version 1)	62
Drinking the Purpose Away (Version 2)	64
Whiskey II	65

DEATH IN THE MIDDLE

Begin Anew	69
My Grandfather's House	73
To Die Broke and Alone	75
The Unremembered	77
You can Imagine	79
Ennui is Death	80
For the Lundy Boys in Remembrance of Major Albro Lynn Lundy, Jr. (1932-1970)	82
Uncle Jim's Last Shot of Whiskey on a Cloudy Day in Late	

September Just Before he was Swallowed by the Earth   84

The Search   86

And death to me   87

An Accident   89

I'm Done   91

Floater   93

THE RISING

Let me Float you a Story   97

The Funeral Director   99

The Thoracic Surgeon   100

Cry for Help   101

Whiskey Dick   102

Family Man   105

Hope Strikes Like Lightning   107

The Disease of our Existence Shrouds the Moon   109

A Legend in the Making   111

The Vow   114

Hair of the Dog   115

Thanksgiving 2005   117

I've Had a Good Life   118

The Rising II   120

RETURN WITH THE ELIXIR

A Few Words of Advice   123

ABOUT THE AUTHOR   125

The Status Quo

It starts at the start
with your future before you
and ends there as well.

MAKE IT A DOUBLE

My first book of poems was so full
of curse words and down and dirty
sex-in-the-milk-cooler imagery
that it was labeled erotica
by the bots at Amazon.com,
not suitable for kids or the elderly or ads.

So, I take a vacuum
to the carpet of its pages
and suck up all the dirty words
and I bend
and lift the used needles
and condoms from its sheets.

I then strip naked,
step into the shower
to scrub the filth off me,
inserting the soap directly
into my mouth and taking special care
not to arouse my man-piece.

But, uncomfortable with the freshly
cleaned and tidied work, I head down
to the Swinging Door Saloon, and goddamn!
Shit! All five-foot-four, 100 pounds of Chenine
is serving behind the bar, so I order

a whiskey neat and, fuck it, make it a double!

ANOTHER GODDAMN SALES MEETING

The statistics are laid out
with great fanfare, a silent pause
dangling at the end of each
for added effect.

They are of great importance,
these statistics, to a small group
of movers and shakers sitting in the front,
nodding their heads after each pause.

And halfway through
the presentation
someone yells from the back,
"Who gives a shit?"

Those words echo off the walls
followed by silence
which, for me at least,
is greatly effective.

WHILING AWAY THE DAY

I while away the day
as Poseidon does,
wade into it
like walking into the cool sea.

I let the seconds rise like water around me,
feel the minutes creep up my skin,
brush up on the hours, feel them
tug at my legs like seaweed.

There is no haste in my day
just as Poseidon does not flit about
nervously, but soaks in time
planning the execution of some great flood,

as an artist takes time to plan his next work,
as I, an unemployed poet, plan
how best to drink time down to its last drop
and cross over to some wiser, wittier place.

CHANNELING BUKOWSKI

I like to channel Bukowski
through the wood panels
at the Swinging Door Saloon
in hopes of gleaning
some of his talent.

Only Hank wasn't much of a fan
of poets like me, so if he shows at all
it's not to help with my prose
but to point his horny soul at
Raven or Thuy or the new girl, Mandy.

I don't judge, Buk.
But how about a little something
for the effort. It's not easy
raising the dead with a simple beer
and the lonesome chant of a lousy drunk.

I Write Love Poems

I write love poems about
wood bars and darkened rooms
ice-cold beer and whiskey.

I cherish the voices of my fellow drunks
and wear the foolishness of their words
like wool around my neck,

our tumblers clanking
like wind chimes
as we toast our luck.

I write about my Uncle and his love
for the drink, his hangovers and mine
shaking hands on the page.

I write of baseball and dirt
my grandparents
Bukowski and cats.

And while I write such things
my wife sits alone at home
patiently waiting for me to return,

perhaps with a poem about her.
But I know in my heart

it is much harder to write

of living loved ones
than of loved ones lost,
those whose souls mix with the smoke

that floats along the bar top
like a hybrid incense of bourbon,
beer and tobacco.

The poet is best when he is most godlike,
taking the black ink of nothing
and shaping it into something memorable.

This is why I write of my fallen kin—
because they are not here anymore
to edit themselves upon the pages of my memory.

They are forever etched there—Hazel,
sucking at her Bushmills, James Patrick, sipping his
St. Pauli and chasing the women around for a kiss.

Meanwhile, my wife waits patiently
at home with Lolo the cat,
eating off a single plate of food.

I am out, of course.
It is Friday night

and I must spend time

with the mistress, booze,
so that there will
continue to be

fire upon the page,
so I can continue to write
anything at all.

Because sober love poems
poems about women, even the ones
you really do love, especially those,

sober love poems about women are prone
to Hallmarkisms, all red rose and chocolate—
they are white wine spritzers

in a whiskey world, and who,
in their right mind would pay
to read shit like that?

HERPES—A LOVE STORY

She had herpes around her
down-there lips
only she called them pimples
but they were herpes
and they made her cry
because no guy would put
his prick there.

But Donny already had herpes
and no other girl would let him
put his thing in them
so, he put it there
and she fell in love with him
and he with her and today
they have four children together.

What's a little weird, though, is that
we were all at the AA reunion yesterday
and still no one wanted to put
their pricks there
and no one wanted his thing in them
even though they both looked great,
even after all these sobering years.

AN ODE TO TITS

Your wife is all
big-fucking-breast—
the kind of breast
that you like to pull from
her spaghetti-string top
and watch plop and fall
to a jiggling stop
over that soft white cotton
with little red cherries
printed on it,
hanging there like a
profound statement,
a poem of great
importance,
giving you pause while,
still in awe of them,
you bend to kiss,
lick and nibble them—
the low-hanging fruit
of the tree of wife.

LIKE A CLOUD IN AUGUST AT NOON

The kitten at the bar doesn't speak English—
I mean, she speaks the language,
just not the clear, multi-syllabic,
simile-laden, poetic English
you prefer to speak,
so you speak gibberish to her
and she responds immediately
bringing your beer
and some food and a tee-shirt
with the bar's new slogan that reads,
"We speak gibberish!"

So, you begin to formulate a plan
to abandon your two degrees
and take up gibberish full time,
only you get home and your wife
doesn't know what the fuck
you're talking about,
so you quiet down,
your words trailing off
like the final notes of a rung bell,
your enthusiasm fading away
like a cloud in August at noon.

SCRATCHING AN ITCH

My cat has nails like sickles
and if you push
on the padded part of his paw
they come out
and are available for inspection.

I stumbled home drunk the other night
and the wife wasn't talking to me,
so I went to where the cat
was napping
and I popped open those claws.

I used them to scratch an itch
on my nose. "Don't touch him, he's filthy!"
my wife yelled from the bed,
and I was glad to know at least
she was still talking to the cat.

DRUNK GENIUS

She deletes my poems
when I pass out at the keyboard
U2 on the CD
cat at my heels
drool snailing its way
down my jaw.

I am a drunk and
she deletes my poems
believing that a drunk is
incapable of genius, otherwise
they would be called genius
instead of drunk.

So, reader, beware the censor—
no matter her intent, she always cuts too deep.

IRON MAN

The warm burn of whiskey
begins in my cheeks
and slowly melts its way down
my chest and arms to my fingertips,
like donning the chainmail
of some great, drunken knight—
one not written about in legend
but who, despite his love for the mead,
was clearly the queen's favorite.

And after a few more shots,
my legs are molten steel,
cooled and hardened
by my chaser of beer, and soon
my beloved appears
out of the shadows, her taut tan body
turning the meat of my groin
into a growing tower,
its steel girders rising toward the sky.

So, I thank you John Powers & Sons,
for this rigid gift of confidence
you have shared with me—
tonight I am hardened,
every challenge this world throws at me,
bouncing off like ping-pong balls

fired against the walls
of the world's strongest skyscraper—
tonight, I am Iron Man.

THESE ARE MY BOOKS

If these were the books
of someone with talent
they would be worth a fortune,
bits of steak fallen from the author's mouth
tucked into the pages
and wedged into the binding
like flecks of gold.

They would turn up one day
in cardboard boxes
and some distant family member
would dig through them
and pull out an old piece of meat
and put it up for sale on eBay
and they would have DNA evidence

that it was once in the author's mouth
and it would sell for a quarter
million dollars
to a dealer of rare books
and the author's work
would see a resurgence
and his heirs would be rich.

But these are my books
and they are worthless—

when you find them
you may as well
just douse them with gasoline
and burn them,
bologna and all.

RUN WITH THE HUNTED

like Bukowski
I run with the hunted.

and though I'm not
the drunkest of drunks
a drunkard is still
a drunkard.

perhaps someday
I'll quit
and wake up each morning
not needing a shit
or to puke.

but until someday comes,
it's the bottle and Buk—
his words and mine
mingling on the page
like drunken rivals at a party,
my lines from the night before
running wild in the margins
throbbing, barking,
a pack of howling dogs,
this empty bottle of Jack
and tattered book of doggerel
reminding me I need to quit—

the writing, not the boozing.

DISAPPOINTMENT

This guy runs over
with his freshly purchased beer
and yells, *Hey, hey!*
That wasn't the winning shot! and
the other guy says, *No shit—but you're
done anyway.* And the guy WAS done,
had four stripes tucked into tough
edges around the table, and Mr. No-Shit
just had the 8, which was teetering
over the hole. And Mr. Done-Guy killed
his beer, made like he was going to take
his shot, then spun and cracked his cue
over Mr. No-Shit's head
and Mr. No-Shit took a knee
and began to bleed down his face
and Mr. Done-Guy fisted the bills
on the table and ran outside
and all I could do
was shake my hanging head,
realizing that round Mr. No-Shit
promised was no longer coming.

CLONE

Writing on the red-neon-lit page
at the Swinging Door Saloon,
balls clacking on the pool table.

A swaying drunk drops a 5 spot
into the juke, and on comes that sweet
Irish soul known as the *Young Dubliners*.

And it's all so terribly right—
the music, the young, ginger bargirl
serving drinks in her Daisy Dukes

and star-spangled bikini top,
the thirty ounces of ice-cold beer
held like a sword in my hand.

And I wonder, ever wish you could
clone your favorite things,
keep the orgasm going indefinitely?

Well, so have I,
and now you know why,
or, at least, what.

The Annoying Guy

I punched him with mighty blows
about his face and I
sent his nose across his cheek
to a new spot under his right eye
and I knuckled his ears
up into his hair
on the top of his head
and broke out all his teeth
leaving him looking like a chewed-up doll.

And my friends called me a pussy
because I didn't knock him out,
but truth is, that guy won't be
going out to the bars
anytime soon on account of his
embarrassing disfigurement—
which is better than flooring him with one blow
only to have him
return tomorrow, wouldn't you agree?

Inventory Shrinkage

You say things to your friends
like, *Hey, Buck Tooth!*
Or, to the fat one,
Hey, Fat Fuck!
And over the next few months—
your finest drinking months ever—
the inventory of people
who like you
has shrunk to record lows.

So, you laugh at the TV
which just reported
on the great economic boom
that has led to overall American
sentiment being at record highs.
Wait 'til they get a load of me, you mutter,
spilling beer down your chest
and staring into the void
of the blackest Friday on record.

Never Trust your Drinking Tutelary in Matters of Life and Death

My guide through the tall grass
was a floating, glowing orb—
which now, in a moment of lucid reflection,
was clearly my Drinking Tutelary.

Yet, even though it had been tasked
with such an important job,
it seemed more concerned that my pants
would fall upon exiting the mud
and muck there in the bar
of the busy theater,
thereby exposing my pruned
white ass and mud-crusted balls,
than it was about the fact that
I had just traversed through six miles
of the cutting blades and brambles
of lush, yet muddy marshland
that formed this waking hallucination,
swatting malarian mosquitoes,
kicking aside alligators and snakes
along the way, or the fact that
this lengthy, painful journey
through nature's minefield
actually ended in the lobby bar
of a grand 1920's era theater,

much less still, the fact that they had
run out of whiskey hours ago
and had just closed out their tills
one minute prior to my emerging
parched and shaking from the wasteland.

THESE GODDAMN HOOPTIES

Cheating spouses are as common
as cars that don't start—
as reliable too.

If only there were a return policy—
we could see them there
back on the lot,
"Price Reduced!" plastered all over them,
"Manager's Special!"

They would be so easy to pass up.

Only, that's not how it works.

Instead, after the prior owners have
finished with them, they are cleaned up
and marketed as one-of-a-kind—
check out the headlights on this one,
that one's rear end has a nice shape to it.

And they are painted in bright
and sexy colors
and all sales are final
and we suckers come along
with a few bucks in our pockets.

28

And we spend the next few decades
watching all hell break loose—
busted hoses and faulty wiring
and cracked engine blocks—
and we wish these fucking things
came with a warning label
or at least a satisfaction guarantee
and a 30-year return policy.

HER EYELASHES

Little come-hither fingers
calling out to their lovers
in black, satin gloves.
One hundred black bodybuilders,
arms flexed and posing
there on the stage
at the end of her eyelids.
A row of German girls
in black sleeves
hoisting full steins of stout
in the middle of Oktoberfest.
Inverted raven claws.
The Congolese Olympic Team
of synchronized swimmers
in the midst of a trick.
Black puffs of smoke from
the red chimney-eye
of a steam engine.

What I mean to say is that
they were long, upward curled
and black...
you know, like one hundred
petrified cat tails
hooked at the ends
and found hanging in a witch's hut.

Beer Battered and Twice Cooked

Cooked, I made my way through
the tall grass like a foul-smelling
animal—
no, not like one.

Cooked, I made my way through
the tall grass, a foul-smelling animal,
sick from too much time
at the watering hole.

I stumbled along like
a wounded beast—
no, I *was* a wounded beast:
circling, self-afflicted, dying.

I saw a light on in a hut
at the edge of the field,
thought it might be home
to the medicine man.

Somehow, I made my way over,
fighting my feet
and gravity,
falling chin-first at his door.

The smell of ground

was familiar,
the clanking of glass coming
from inside was as well.

Shit, I said to no one, *I'm back
where I started*—the bar with
the witch, and her bottles, and her friends
with their long nails and little eyes.

Welcome back, I heard one say.
Let's batter him and throw him onto the fire,
another muttered under her breath,
I bet he tastes delicious.

THIS WHOLE FILTHY WORLD

The world slithers along
on its filthy gut.

Nuns lie, wives lie
even mothers lie.

Everyone lies to sell their story
to get more shit

to make friends
to frighten enemies.

So, you end your life with a razor—
you slip away

all sticky and bloody
into the other world

where people
give it to you straight

where even the witches
look you in the eye

as they tell you just how much
this is going to hurt

before muttering their incantations
and changing you into a snake.

A Simple "thank you" Would Have Sufficed

You search for the right word—
the sensitive, witty one,
wise as go-go boots
with miniskirts.
You dig and dig, tug as though
your best friend is dangling
on the other end of the rope,
his feet blistering
from a river of lava
that is rising ever higher from below,
and you yank with all your might
and out he pops.

But it is too late and Mandy
has delivered your beer and left
and you look at the word you excavated
and it is neither witty nor wise,
just some article or pronoun,
a pair of fists around a rope,
white knuckles and tendon,
your best friend absorbed by the fire,
your favorite bargirl gone away
without any of your words
beating in her heart,
not even "Thank you."

CONVERSATION WITH A FRIEND

is
very
     drunk
worse
          than
   just a
little
     drunk?

probably
          not;
     maybe so.
i'm
          not sure.
     i'll let
you know
     tomorrow.

Eighty Dollars Ago

Eighty dollars ago
I was somewhat charming
and capable of witty banter.

But three rounds and six fingers
of whiskey later, I am just
a potbellied man teetering on his stool,

cursing the gods
for this horrible trick
they've inflicted on my life,

hoping the twenty I stuck
in the margins of my book hours ago
is still there.

Eighty dollars ago
my name was Jackson P. Falldrecker
square-jawed, majesty-man from Mississippi.

Now, I am just Randy in the corner,
eighty dollars in the hole
and in great danger of losing my mind.

AGING

The years shuffle off
like guests insulted at a party—
slow and grumbling, their pockets
full of your fondest memories.

THE DESCENT

The descent into
the innermost cave always
begins with whiskey.

WHISKEY I

The whiskey weighs on me
like a leaden cloak
leaching into my bloodstream,
changing the very structure
of my face.

It is like tying cannonballs
to my cheeks
with fishhooks and fishing line.
It makes my eyes sag and my smile
look like a warped door.

But it is still
the surest bet I know
for making it through the day,
and well worth all this
embarrassing disfigurement.

CONSUMPTION

I sip my beer
more slowly now,
like a man
with consumption
sucking at his cough syrup.

I am an old, sick man
nipping at the medicine,
prolonging my days
but no longer
enjoying them.

LOSERS LIKE US

Ever been too drunk?
For too long?
The idiot? Not tall enough?
Not smart enough? Rich enough?
Your car too hooptie?
Girls don't like you?
You don't like you?

Good, then you and I
are kindred souls.

You and I are the limp dickweeds
in a field of rigid, glowing cocks,
our minds too small,
our dreams too big,
our balls not substantial enough.

We bring down the curve.

We make drivel a national language,
only the nation we live in
has no need for language,
no storytellers recalling our great wars,
and the victories we celebrate
are false victories
with false heroes, false heroines.

We have no rock striking at flint
to spark the kindling of our thoughts,
no lanterns of hope lighting
the walkways of our minds,
no beautiful women
banging at our doors at 1am.

So, forgive me, partner
for purposefully drinking too much
with you today
at the Swinging Door Saloon
and for taking my keys with me
as I exit the bar.

It is my intention to leave us both
high and dry, my smoking,
wrecked car the last thing
either of us remember about
this embarrassingly inadequate life.

I CRIED TODAY

Quite near 3:30 in the morning
I awoke shaking and wet with sweat,
my pillows, a couple
dampened dogs beneath me.

I wasn't exactly sure where I was
until I heard the familiar snore
of the woman I love
roaring through the dark.

I suddenly felt something stir—
the pain of our missing cat,
or the neighbor's dog
dead beneath my car.

So, I quickly pushed aside the pillows
tore away the sheets and ran to the can
where I knelt before the toilet
and gave my guts to the bowl.

And amid all the retching,
I became aware of some briny tears
squeezed out of the sac there
in the clit-shaped corner of my eye.

So, reader, please do not think me

uncouth, uncaring, unfeeling.
Because, baby, I feel things
deeply, right from the gut.

HERE'S WHAT YOU SHOULD DO

You should rescue the kitten,
or stop global warming,
or create an interesting new cracker.

You should make candy
that fights tooth decay,
guacamole that melts off the pounds.

You should make
roses that grow thorn-free, and beer
that brings you closer to your goals.

You should stop a forest fire
and war, and the onset
of disease.

You should take the fluttering,
injured bird off the garden floor
and put it in a shoe box to keep it going.

You should make kindergarten
the new college and obesity
a means to healthy living.

You should make husbands
love their wives, and wives

47

make good on their promises.

There are many things you should do,
but you don't. You just keep doing
what you're doing—drink, drank, drunk.

Meanwhile, the schoolkids grow
to hate their schools and start wars,
the bird dies, and the fires spread.

But what should really concern you
is the kitten in the coyote's mouth,
and your wife no longer answering your calls.

A LONELY DRUNK

Ninety ounces in, a fly buzzes my ear
completes a couple sorties around my mug
before finally landing atop the sticky table
right next to my cell phone. It was clear
he just wanted some of my spilled beer,
so he and I were clearly likeminded creatures.

Still, I was going to crush him with
my book just for the sport of it.

But as I raised my journal above my head,
I realized that I loved him, he being
my only remaining drinking buddy,
and not wanting to risk
any more spilled beer,
I backed off,
lifting my other hand off the table,
and the lack of my weight
made it wobble
and my cell phone started to slide
and the little fucker flew off.

It's been a couple hours now
and I kind of wish I had squashed him
on account of my being
so goddamn lonely.

Negative Self-Talk #1

You can write poems along the water in Balboa
with the wind bending back the palm trees
like a college boy bends back the legs of a coed.

And you can sound out the words as the wind
makes whistling sounds over your bottle of beer.

You can even tell the devil your soul is his.

But you will never find reward with your pen,
you stupid, scribbling, soulless hack!

Negative Self-Talk #2

Well, aren't you just so special?
You with your thinning hair
and mysterious clicking hip?

You fancy yourself an original thinker,
but your neanderthal thoughts fall out
of your head like young children

fall out of bed, startled and crying,
confused, not at all sure whether
or not they're still dreaming.

You were not always so hard on the eyes,
the doggerel of hard living not yet
scribbled all over your face.

I've seen pictures so I know it's true.
But that was so long ago
it's hardly worth mentioning here.

And, while I seem to recall
a rather funny knock-knock joke
you told back in the 3rd grade,

let me tell you something, pal,
it's been nothing but a quiet,

smoky room ever since,

your joke bombs concussing
an uncomfortable audience
that clamors for its money back.

You'd think the years would have been
kinder to you, would have taught you something
but you are an ugly, confused dolt.

And every time I come to you
for answers, it's like
breaking bones to find one.

I hate to say it, buddy,
but you may as well pack it in, because
this whole "You Show" is not working out.

TROUBLE IS BREWING

I've slid comfortably
right into a
third beer
after having
sworn an oath
over a napkin bible
on a Formica altar
to stop at two.

Bukowski
used to run with interesting bums
but he got old
and moneyed
and he began
to eat healthy
and sleep indoors
with a respectable woman.

I am working it backwards,
forcing the respectable to sleep alone
while I settle in under the stars
in a strawberry field in Irvine,
passing wine around with a couple pickers
as they say things in Spanish
I don't understand and give me looks
that indicate trouble is brewing.

OUR HEADS INTO THE MOUTH OF THE BEAST

Lion tamers do it,
knowing they won't be bitten.

I saw a crocodile hunter do it, albeit
to a toothless crock.

There was even a Russian
with a very thick skull
who lay his on the pillow
of an old bear's tongue
as if to nap there until springtime.

But you and I do it with more at stake,
with wives expecting us home by midnight
wives armed with knives
and legal documents
and angry words
like *divorce* and *child support*,
their teeth sharpened
by half of everything we own.

There are bosses with whiskey-sniffing noses
and crushing jaws, with a lust for
chewing us up in front of the staff.

The police circle, bouncers leer,

kickboxers and wrestlers
wait for us to insult their intelligence,
so they can separate us from our limbs
before beating their chests,
grabbing their balls
and slipping out the back door
with our wallets and wives.

And still we order the bartender
to bring the beast over.

We open its mouth and stick our heads in
savoring the smell of its sweet breath
and staring down its throat like
a suicide staring into
the barrel of a shotgun.

We then climb in and devour it whole
from the inside out
before staggering home like a cave man
who'd slain a mammoth
with nothing more than some courage
and a love for the taste of its blood.

THE DIRTY RAG OF LIVING

I try to make good choices—
doughnuts with my nieces
even though I'm trying to lose weight,
coffee with my parents
regardless of its effects on my colon.
I choose my nephew's Pony League game
instead of the Million Dollar Derby
at Santa Anita. But inevitably,
there will be that Saturday night
before Mother's Day,
when I will be passed out in a bush
beside the railroad tracks
and I won't get up for the family brunch,
which starts at 10, won't get up until noon
when the Surfliner roars by
with all the mothers aboard staring out at me
with judging eyes
as I rise to my feet, my clothes full of foxtails
and drag my ass home—
a million good choices
wiped clean with the dirty rag of living.

THE BIGGEST DRUNK I EVER MET

The biggest drunk I ever met
drove my car and banged my wife
in the back of it.

He had the same haircut as me
and spoke with all the same inflections
and the same lack of meaning.

The biggest drunk I ever met
was a pretty good guy
most of the time.

So, when he told me to fuck off and die
one day at work, I let him off with a warning
and walked him down to the Door

to buy him a shot of bourbon.
But the bartender
could not see him standing there

with me, so I drank his shot along with
mine and I called his girlfriend at home
and told her she should come down here

and have some fun with me
in the back of her boyfriend's car

and I started to get a little horny

at the thought of it.
Then his girlfriend asked me
what the fuck I was talking about

and did I need a ride home
and by the way, did I remember
to pay the mortgage?

48 Hours in the Tank

You can't find sobriety
in a piece of meat.
Even with
the beans and rice,
it's just a piece of meat—
no more capable
of turning you into
a serious man
than coffee at 3am,
or fresh air
on the long drive home,
or a toilet that flushes
your insides away,
or, as some of us have tried,
48 hours in the tank.

MY WIFE

My wife could gut me
and sell the sedan
and burn my books
and stuff my corpse
with pinecones
and prop me up in the yard
beneath the olive tree
to keep the crows off the lawn.

She wouldn't, she says,
but she most murderously
and certainly could—
if so inclined,
if pushed too hard.

SHE IS THE DAWN

When she is coming,
she is dawn
breaking over a distant hill.

When she is walking away
she is nightfall
on a night you have nothing—
no address to go home to,
no tent, no pillow, no jokes
not one goddamn thing to pass out with
in the middle of your greatest drunk.

She is your wife.

And without her
you don't even have the fear of death
without which
there is no going on.

Drinking the Purpose Away (Version 1)

The drunk in the bar,
drank all his liquor and that
of the black folk, and the whites
and the Uzbeks, and the Eskimos
and he drank the very purpose out of the day
making that bar
a blackhole of fecklessness
a word his fellow drunks have trouble with
when sober, much less now
at closing.

And he wonders what happened to them
as they sit there staring at ghosts
their sandwiches still uneaten
in metal lunchboxes atop the bar
their papers unread and folded
in the corner
their spent cigarettes
littering the parking lot out back
like a thousand distant suns
on the black sky of asphalt,
their cell phones
buzzing with messages
in coat pockets
in glove compartments
and under seats

and beneath the strawberries
in the field he will sleep in
until the unnatural light
of the police cruiser spots him
and the batons poke him
and the questions come at him
like bullets
entering his head
like matter into the void
where they will die
unanswered
one on top of the other
like the strength of youth
like one's purpose
like dreams
like hope
like me.

Drinking the Purpose Away (Version 2)

The drunk drinks all his liquor
and that of his neighbors at the bar
and of the suits that left
their whiskies neat on the pool table
to take their cigarette breaks
and phone calls outside.

And the drunk drinks
his very purpose away,
even drinking it out of the pretty
girl with big tits and tight ass
who would be a savage in bed
if he hadn't drunk his cock into slumber,
so he takes inventory
and, seeing a dismal future,
he drinks one for the road
exits her apartment and
walks into the biting cold,
heading northeast into the storm
his head bowed by the wind,
and he continues walking,
walking, walking further
away from home, headed
for that final bit of peace and quiet
there in the frigid valley of emptiness.

WHISKEY II

Oh, liquid courage
liquid death
devil in a bottle.

Crown Prince of Low-Life
you fluid killer
of Hope.

What gives you the right
to take from me
all that I've worked for?

Who handed you
the parchment
inked with my name?

Where did these waves
of whiskey-driven madness
originate?

Was it not you
who whispered promises
of strength and originality?

Was it not you who then
snatched the marrow from my skull

and replaced it with Absurdite?

Surely you have better things
to do than to toy with me
you giant cat's paw of murder.

Why not just end it already?
Pull the goddamn trigger!
Finish me.

DEATH IN THE MIDDLE

Everyone must die.
It's the natural order.
So please, Love, don't cry.

She will be painting over a lone chip
in her nails and drinking wine one day
at the tennis club while watching
her new husband play racquetball,
and her server will return
to ask her how she wanted
her steak cooked.

And that one word, "steak"
will instantly transport her
back to life with me,
Poet Laureate of the Absurd,
founder of Bits of Steak Press,
her first true love and father
to her only son.

And she will
remember our unique love
and some of the difficult days
as well and she will
mutter *rare* as the tears
swell in her eyes,
so very, very rare.

BEGIN ANEW

I.

My Wife Ex Post Facto

After the big heart boom boom
(that's what I like to call my eventual
catastrophic heart attack)
she will cry every day for a week
and 3 days more.

On the 11th day, she will have a nice breakfast
and a fast-paced comedy in the evening.
She will wake up on the 12th day
and realize she didn't cry for the first time
and that realization will make her cry.

But she will wake up on the 13th day
and turn on the news
and begin painting her nails
and the cat will jump up on the bed
and she will feed it breakfast.

That night, she will order a pizza
drink one of my leftover beers
which she will find
in the back of the fridge

behind the teriyaki sauce she bought for the wake.

She will cry a little then, but it will be light
and she will quickly recover.
The coming months will be drier still
and the years as well and she will
make new friends and quit talking to mine.

And my pictures will be sold
on Craig's List because someone
from Santa Ana needed a frame
and I will look down on things
from the cloudy saloon of heaven.

And the only thing that will remain
is that beautiful girl
I left behind there on the day
the final period was typed
at the end of our love story.

II.

My Wife 7 Years Ex Post Facto

She's painted her nails red
got a butterfly tattoo
on her ass—
my wife,

7 years after
my heart attack.

I saw her yesterday
in a drunken dream,
as she wantonly lived out
the fantasies that built up
during our marriage,
her hands clutching
the pillow,
those red nails glowing,
her ass in the air
like a stink bug,
that butterfly tattoo
flapping its wings,
begging for the pearls
of another man's cock.

I think I will lay off the whiskey
and increase my daily dose of fiber
and begin eating broccoli—
I'd suddenly like to live and
I don't like what my current diet
is doing to me.

III.

My Wife 20 Years Ex Post Facto

MY GRANDFATHER'S HOUSE

My grandfather's house will be sold
and the new owners will
knock out walls
and gut rooms
they will remove trees
and pare down the bushes
I hid things in as a child.

But for now, this small bungalow
on Beachwood
below the Hollywood sign
still conducts its symphony—
branches on rain gutters,
pipes humming with the flow of water,
wooden floors creaking,
the sound
a sort of muffled clicking
like an old man with bad knees
taking a walk through the mud.

These sounds enter my room
like heavy news
that takes time to sink in.

Through the windows
the wind blows

the old house cleans its instruments
readying itself
for the evening performance
its last in the series
and some would say
its most forlorn
and memorable.

TO DIE BROKE AND ALONE

I wonder about my
true reserves of strength.

I *think* I can handle
being broke and hungry
and alone
in the alleys of America,
writing stories of survival
on cardboard,
living off pickle juice
and discarded bread.

But sometimes I think
I might get desperate
and start robbing people
on their way out of McDonald's
stealing their wallets
and Happy Meals,
eating their burgers
in front of their children
and selling their Happytoys
to tourists downtown.

Either way, I'd like to think
I have what it takes
to die broke

and toothless,
alone and wet in an alley,
only a pen to my name,
the story of my life
scribbled incoherently
on the walls
of my cardboard home.

The Unremembered

Not all of us get photographed
with our feet up on the dashboard,
cowboy hat cocked atop
our perfectly coifed heads
our best features
profiled
for young American women
to fall in love with.

We do not die in Porsches
tumbling into the memory books
best feature flipping over
best feature
with news crews dispatched to the scene.

Most of us just die of cancer
or diabetes or liver failure,
all guts, no glory,
no legacy,
no lasting beauty,
no scrap metal on display
as a cautionary tale to young drivers,
no pretty girls leaving
flowers on our grave.

Most of us end up

planted face up
in the dirt
in a quiet ceremony
on a rainy day
unremembered,
our best feature, our ability
to roll with it all until
it rolls all over us.

You can Imagine

You read in the inflight magazine
that in ballet, it is the males
which are most impressive—
higher leaps, longer jumps,
the pure athleticism—
you can just imagine them
out on the tarmac
on your way out of Newark
dancing like it's the last day
of their lives,
all arabesque and assemblé
as they grand jeté into the turbine
of your taxiing 777
the bloody, bony,
meaty fruits
of their gracefulness
spraying
out the back of the jet engine
like a human shaved ice.

You *can* imagine that,
can't you?

Ennui is Death

Ennui is death, not just
to the poet, but also to the poem.

—McNair

Four beers in—nothing.
Not a single bit worth saving.
Words, yes, but none
that weep or laugh
or drive trains into
oncoming trains
or cars into brick walls,
no bodies sent hurtling
through the windshield as the horn
wails and the tires screech.

Just words, brown ones, inspiring
as dead leaves in a gardener's sack.

I watch the bargirls slide by,
intent on their work. I suppose
they are beautiful. It is hard to say,
having no strange fantasies about them,
no unusual desire. And it dawns on me,
this is why I prefer writing at
the strip club or funeral parlor

or Billy Collins reading.
The writing, like the living,
is so much better when you feel something,
anything—lust, sadness, envy—
it does not matter,
just something, some reminder
that death has no power over you
yet.

FOR THE LUNDY BOYS IN REMEMBRANCE OF MAJOR ALBRO LYNN LUNDY, JR. (1932-1970)

The characters of war
in their youth
had forgettable names—
no Rickenbackers, Rommels
or Pattons.
MacArthur left no tobacco
on the battlefields of their minds,
Montgomery no Union Jacks.

And who in hell's name was Ho Chi Minh?

No, they were just boys.

Instead they had Schlatters
and Schmidts, Trujillos
and bloody McNairs
lying in wait
in the white-dirt ditches of the chalkfields
there in Rancho Palos Verdes.

They were just boys
but they fought ferociously
lobbing dirt clods like grenades,
stabbing each other with sticks,
pelting themselves with pebbles

like machine gun fire.

So, when they played
with their little green army men
they gave them heroic, memorable names.

Beowulf took a bullet
in the Hell of Vons Hill.

Hercules squished an entire enemy battalion
between his finger and thumb
in the fight to take Ridgecrest Road.

There was Timmy the Saber,
his right arm removed
a bayonet taped there in its place,
who single-handedly
won the Battle for Big Gulley.

But when their father didn't report back
for Christmas in 1970
there was a massacre on the coffee table
all one hundred fifty friendlies lost
all of them Majors,
all of them named Albro Lynn Lundy, Jr.

Uncle Jim's Last Shot of Whiskey on a Cloudy Day in Late September Just Before he was Swallowed by the Earth

I take pictures of my whiskey and beer
in their tiny glass houses
and the snow-frosted chalets of their mugs—
it soothes me,
they are like little souvenirs,
trinkets that I collect while traveling.

And I title the pictures
with lengthy descriptors
to give them deeper meaning.

Like,
Shots in Scottsdale
prior to my arrest
in the fountain
and,
Pitcher killed in 25 seconds
left-handed after softball game in Chico
prior to my arrest in the park.

I've saved these photos on my computer
and a program cycles them through
in three second intervals.

Occasionally I'll hit the space bar
and the picture freezes and
I'll sit there staring for moments on end
as I tug on my beer thinking,
perhaps I love these mementos
a little too much.

But they are the postcards
and refrigerator magnets
of my journey into the drink
and they carry great emotion,
like the one I took on a cloudy day
in late September
of a shooter of Jack Daniels
that shone like an umber section
of stained glass
from a fractured beam of sunlight
that had hit it just so.

And behind the glass
an arrangement of flowers—
the whole scene peaceful as any painting
there on the lid of my Uncle's casket
just before he was swallowed by the earth.

THE SEARCH

Tap the keg—
nothing.
Kill the whiskey—
nothing.
Jump the rich guy—
nothing.
Ride the sexy bargirl—
nothing.
Flip the switch
and pull the lever—
nothing.
Pour out the sour milk—
nothing.
Search the house—
nothing.
Check the trunk of your car—
nothing.
But open the coffin
and there she is—
Joy,
foul-smelling and stiff
and just as beautiful
as you remembered.

AND DEATH TO ME

death to the goatee
and man blouse.

death to sunglasses
worn in dark bars.

death to wobbly bar stools
and warm beer.

death to cliché.

death to cavities, cancer
and the word "rectum."

death to the zoo—I say
let the animals run loose in the streets.

death to aging.

death to the short lives of pets.

death to black and white,
except as it relates
to good and evil.

death to the liar, cheat

and coward.

death to deadlines
and middle management.

death to time clocks
and uncomfortable shoes.

death to worrying how you look.

death to judgment.

death to worry.

death to Tax Day and taxes
and congressmen who write the laws.

death to all of it—
this poem, the last one,
and the ones before that.

death to every miserable thing.
and death, of course, to me.

An Accident

I fear I'm going to accidentally
hang myself from an oak tree
by flukily attaching
my least favorite ties around my neck
and, not by purpose
but by some awful twist of fate,
attaching the other end of those ties
to a branch and, again,
completely without premeditation,
climb onto that branch
and sit there reviewing the knots,
and with everything attached properly
lose my balance
and slip off like some fool
in a dunking booth.

I will hang there, feet dangling
above the flowerbed,
a dead man strung from
an oak tree
in the middle of town
early on a Sunday morning.

And as you drive home from church
and discover me there
swaying in the breeze,

take a moment to drink it in.

I think you will come to appreciate
one of nature's
most bizarre accidents.

I'M DONE

The power has been cut off
the machines are still
and the calliope no longer plays.

The carnival—
this freak show of my life—
is over.

I pet the frozen horse
on the carousel
and walk the black pavement
alone
bits of trash drifting at my side.

Out there in the night
the bearded lady laughs and
the midgets dance and sing while
the strong man rips a piece of steel from
the tiger's cage and bends it into a noose.

And soon, from a bush,
the tiger emerges
his glowing eyes growing larger
and LARGER
with each mighty step.

Tomorrow, when the news crews arrive
they will find me strung
from the gallows of the Ferris wheel
my body chewed up and frozen,
my neck twisted and broken
in its metal halter
my legs bent into a sitting posture
and, as the cameras zoom in,
they will see the great black
dwarf of death
sitting there in my lap
smiling, his top hat tilted forward,
smoke wafting from his pipe
his sharp yellow teeth glowing
like stars
from the black hole of his mouth
as he reads the story of my life
out loud
those dull, forgettable
forty-two chapters
of nothing.

FLOATER

I am overtaken.

Over, like the rolling of credits
with no sequels planned.

Taken, like a drunk guy
at a whorehouse.

I am done, swollen,
a floater's gassy body
stuck in the delta reeds.

I am a drunk in a sober world—
nothing to hide behind
but a beer-stained napkin
with a few incoherent words
written on it. That,
and the good word of people who knew me
when I mattered
when my thirst for life was still unquenched
when I hadn't yet cashed in my future
like an addict
with a stolen check.

I am overtaken. Done.
Let my obituary make note of this day,

let the death certificate show
the cause of death as too much living,
carve my headstone with the following:

He lived so much, it killed him.

The Rising

Elevate your mind
lift your chin, stand up and walk
back toward daylight.

LET ME FLOAT YOU A STORY

They had me spring off
the diving board
on account of my prowess
on the baseball field.

But I knew of no
professional baseball players
who were also divers, so I hit up
my parents' liquor cabinet first.

And on my first spring
I just kept rising and rising, above
my mom who flailed and jumped
in her attempt to keep me grounded.

Above my dad who, believing in
tough love, just watched me
keep rising with that sad,
knowing look fathers are famous for.

And I kept on rising
and rising
above the lifeguard tower
above the roof of the pool house

and the olive tree

and the redwoods and the clouds
and the curvature of the earth
and once I passed the sun

I stopped in to drink some
whiskey and beer
with the gods and, screw it,
make it a double!

And while I'm sad about
my parents' suffering
over my slow rising
away from them,

at least I have this story to share
with you all,
and you know how
we drunks love our stories.

THE FUNERAL DIRECTOR

As the guests
walked into
the parlor

the funeral
director
stumbled

uncontrolled
and cursing
into

his client's casket
wherein lied
his fate.

THE THORACIC SURGEON

Old fella swallowed his bourbon awkwardly
and an ice cube lodged sideways
in his throat. He became flustered
all waving arm and pounding fist.

The bargirl wanted to call 911
but the drug dealers wouldn't have it.

So, I stood on my barstool
and announced to the entire bar
that I was a thoracic surgeon
and that this fellow would be fine
since the ice cube would surely melt
and his breathing return to normal
before the lack of oxygen
did any lasting damage.

With that,
the bar became settled again
save the choking guy in the corner
who just couldn't stop waving his arm
and pounding his fist, regardless of the fact
that I was a thoracic surgeon
and that the ice cube would surely melt
eventually.

CRY FOR HELP

You languish in your job
unhappy, trapped, unhinged
cursing the gods for your horrible existence
in a pitiful cry for help.

So, they come down on lit chariots
steeds snorting and kicking
and they find you naked on the floor
of your kitchen, passed out,
the handle to the refrigerator in one hand,
a bologna sandwich in the other.

You are nothing,
one of them whispers into your ear
as you slowly awaken
and rise to your feet
pulling lettuce from your teeth.

Oh really? you reply,
wondering how many other men
have the gods themselves
bearing down on them in burning chariots,
their horses snorting
like you are Hades himself.

WHISKEY DICK

Right in the middle of it all
it begins to feel too small
for the job and, thinking that,
it begins to shrink—
the power of negative thinking.

Before long, he is not even
hitting the sides much less
bottoming out and soon the battle is lost,
his defeated private
plopping out to a whoosh of air to lie there
sticky and wet against his leg.

The curtains rustle in the gentle breeze
and a soft glow creeps in
from the street below,
as she lies staring into the night,
unconquered, wondering as he does,
"What kind of man is this?"

So, he begs her pardon,
rolls over and reaches under the bed
for his jet pack
which he stores there
for just such occasions,
and, bidding adieu,

he rockets naked out his window
streaking across the midnight sky
to his secret cave
in the side of the Santa Ana Mountains.

There, he lights a small fire and takes up
the lost art of hieroglyphics.
He draws himself on a hilltop
his cock wrapped twice around his waist,
then down his left leg
in serpentine fashion,
and he draws it laid out on the ground
like a fire hose around his feet,
and he keeps drawing,
making it rise above his head
like a long-necked dinosaur,
and he draws a young woman there
her legs spread just so,
the head of his serpent
wrapping around her shoulders
and down between her breasts,
her eyes round and ready,
her awestruck face
smiling in the firelight.

In 2000 years, when the new explorers
come and discover his cave
they will find his drawings

and they will give him a name
and start a new religion in his honor
and they will spread the good news
across the land
and all of humankind will finally know
just what kind of man he was.

FAMILY MAN

I'm sitting on the curb talking with
a homeless man
about his wife and kids
and what the hell happened to put him here
alone on the street
bumming cigarettes and beer from
drunks like me
who still have cars and homes
and wives. There are no answers
he decides, just actions and results,
good times and bad. I nod as we
share our brown-bagged bottle beneath the stars.

Soon, my wife stands at our side
and shares the old man's cigarette.
He and I swill our juice
and watch my wife
sway beneath the streetlight
as if she's listening to music,
orange ribbon fluttering from her hair,
her blouse open just so,
a soft smile stuck to her face.

I can't help but love
these moments,
sitting on street corners,

feeling the warmth of liquor in my blood,
feeling my wife in there too,
and John, the homeless guy—
all of us riding this booze-fueled ride together
not worrying about tomorrow,
deciding instead
to live this moment as family,
come what may.

HOPE STRIKES LIKE LIGHTNING

How do I make it?

I wait the fucker out
keep knocking 'em back
to see what happens.

Maybe the sugary lotto ball
of Death
will fall in my lap mid sip
one lucky Saturday evening
and I will be electrocuted
and explode
like a lightning strike
to a giant transformer.

And this dirty old town
and all the universe
will see my light
and little planetary beings
will study me, and say
their alien prayers for my soul.

And I will become solid again
in some giant paradise
where drinks are waiting for me.

And women and dead pets.

And rocky trails will suddenly appear
rising into the clouds
where I eat bologna sandwiches
and fuck
and lie around
and read a detailed story
about the amazing death
of an average drunk
which brought light to
a dirty, Earth town
to the entire universe
one lucky Saturday evening.

THE DISEASE OF OUR EXISTENCE SHROUDS THE MOON

The disease of our existence
shrouds the moon
cloaks the sun
wraps a warm cape
around the stars.

Our universe
is being reigned in,
God's arm around our shoulder—
lights out, game over.

No more Mars Rover.

We've reached out as far
as we're going to.

Time to sit down
in the office and learn
our fate. Promotion
or no, it's been
a good fight.

Let judgment come.

I, for one, will not be ashamed

as I lock eyes
and hear the news.

A Legend in the Making

All aboard the drunk train to Nowheresville
with the muses stoking the fire
up on their bouncy chairs,
their glorious bumps jiggling as they
pull the levers and twist the knobs,
while the gatekeepers
make sure this fucking thing
stays on the tracks.

Doesn't matter if we end up Nowhere,
they say. *Just keep 'er on the tracks.*

There are a great many poets on board
and they write neatly
on the tidy pages
of their leather-bound journals
in their air-cooled cars
and they finish their odes
and sonnets about their
one true loves
and run them up to the gatekeepers
in the steaming locomotive.

They genuflect and raise the poems
with bowed heads and loose wrists
and the gatekeepers take them

and scan them for grammar
and to make sure the fucking things
stay on track.

These are the well-mannered writers
who keep on submitting
to the gatekeepers, to their publishers
and to their one true loves
and to their true loves' girlfriends
and to their true loves' boyfriends
on bended knees
and most of their poems get the green
check mark
and make it into the mailbag
which gets hung on the hook
at 35 miles per hour
and they make it to the editors
with those green
check marks
and articles are written
about such beautifully
submissive work.

Meanwhile, back on the train,
I refuse to submit and
I carry a dozen poems
and a bottle of Jack
up to the front

and my shirt is untucked
and my hair uncombed
and my poems are summarily
tossed into the fire
for getting off track,
for being smudged with the soot
of hard living
and for not mentioning
my one true love by name.

And judging by the looks of
the polished poets as I pass by,
you'd think I was a chainsaw killer
or wheelchair thief
if not for a few of the older muses
seeing my whiskey and inviting me up
to their chairs
to touch their various bumps, knobs
and levers by the fire.

Once again in my life,
there by the heat of the firebox
I find myself drunk, wild-eyed
and erect, and not the least bit
concerned about publication.

THE VOW

It's Monday
and the son enters first and orders
for his mother and himself—
a tall Budweiser and double Jack
on the rocks. She chain-smokes
out back, leaning into her cane
and muttering like a witch
in the middle of a spell.

Eventually,
she'll fag out and enter the bar
sitting on the stool her boy
has prepared for her.
I watch them
from against the wall
where I match them
drink for drink.

By the time
her teeth have slipped the gums
and fallen
into her 6th bucket of Jack
and her boy has passed out
in the van parked outside,
I've vowed for the 1,645th time
never to drink again.

HAIR OF THE DOG

The kindly gentleman behind the bar
offered me some hair of the dog that bit me,
my face clearly telling the tale
of the night before,
when, while drinking alone in a dark bar
somewhere in Hollywood,
out of the blue, I was viciously attacked
by some sick-looking dog,
its words harsh and unforgiving,
its vocabulary better than mine,
its elocution also,
its coral-sharp fangs cutting through my flesh
like an axe through a piece of rice paper,
its hungry jaws digging into my guts
like a stray into its first-ever bowl of meat,
its foul breath stealing the life from my lungs,
leaving my brain sore from a lack of oxygen.

So, I order a water
and walk back to my table.

No, I don't remember a word that dog said,
but, although the gentleman behind the bar
looks kindly enough, I think
I've learned my lesson—
that when it comes to drinking,

you'd best steer clear of the dogs altogether,
not to mention the ones whose job it is
to feed them.

THANKSGIVING 2005

Had lunch with my bride
in the cafeteria at Irvine Regional Hospital.
As an employee, hers was free.
Mine cost $17.
The turkey was processed, but salt-free.
The yams were cold
but tasted like cherry pie.
The mashed potatoes came in a bowl
and had the consistency of grits.
The peas were good though.
And my wife was smiling.
So, in case I die before the day is over,
let these lines document that I crossed over
hungry, my wallet a little bit lighter,
but with a smiling wife—
a true Thanksgiving blessing.

I'VE HAD A GOOD LIFE

Check it out.
Do your research.
Call the record keepers,
summon the temperature takers,
pull the gauge readers from their gauges.

I've had a good life.

There have been missteps, sure,
scabs that tore off
old wounds that bled through
and stained my jeans,
broken bones that did not mend straight.

But it has not been all bankruptcy and bad health
as the papers would have you believe.

I have had a very good life—
kittens, mud, sacramental wine, first kisses,
views up a schoolgirl's skirt.
It has been good strawberries mixed with
chocolate liqueur, whiskey with my beer,
beds to sleep in when tired.

I have a beautiful wife and brilliant boy.

Sure, I have seen many jail cells
been awakened on tumbleweeds
and playgrounds
and underneath trucks
and not known how I got there.

Yes, I've been called *Drunk*
in Russian, Gaelic and Chinese
and all the major Romance languages.

But I have saved half eaten-humming birds
from my cat and nursed them back to life,
given XXL underwear to fat homeless people
and stroked the head of a dying dolphin
giving it some peace in it's final seconds.

These things matter too.

It has not been all bad.

I've had a good life.

You can look it up.

Or maybe,
you can just take my word for it.

THE RISING II

I've burned it all down
The good, the bad—now it's time
I rise from the ash.

Return with the Elixir

The fight for my life
would be so boring without
this constant learning.

A Few Words of Advice

So, my strange reader-friend,
what have I learned
from my exploits
with the bottle?

Three things:

One: every drunk should have Life Alert—
for those common occasions when
you've fallen and can't get up.
Two: cherish life's small moments—
they are the reward of a well-lived life.
Three: be true to your spouse—
otherwise, what's the point?

Oh, and never give a chainsaw
to a monkey.

So, four things.
I've learned four things
from my exploits with the bottle.

Make that five: never enter
the Swinging Door Saloon
without a pen—it will be
of little use in the event

of a knife fight, but of every
benefit when you awaken alone
in some strange field without
the slightest idea how you got there.

ABOUT THE AUTHOR

Described by his inner circle as Poet Laureate of the Absurd, Randall McNair spent the better part of a decade drinking himself silly at the Swinging Door Saloon in Tustin, California. While there, he was inspired to put pen to paper by a combination of Charles Bukowski, Billy Collins, Sharon Olds and the muse at large. McNair is the award-winning author of Dispatches from the Swinging Door Saloon and his poems have been printed in both American and Canadian literary journals. He lives in Alameda, California with his wife and young son. You can view some of his more current work at: https://www.mcnairpoet.com/blog and his books are available for purchase at barpoems.com.